What's in Reading Practice at Home?

A Story for Each Letter of the Alphabet!

There are both fiction and nonfiction stories in *Reading Practice at Home*. Each one-page story has full-color pictures to help beginning readers.

The activity pages that follow each story provide practice with comprehension, letter sounds, sequencing, and a variety of other age-appropriate prereading and reading skills.

Practice Cards

Pages 145–160 contain letter and picture cards for reading practice. You will find suggestions for using the cards on pages 3 and 4.

How to Use Reading Practice at Home

Provide Time

Make sure that your child has a quiet time for practice. The practice session should be short and successful. Consider your child's personality and other activities as you decide how to schedule daily practice periods.

Provide Materials

Put extra writing and drawing paper, scissors, crayons, pencils, and a glue stick in a tub or box. Store the supplies and *Reading Practice at Home* in the work area you and your child choose.

Provide Encouragement and Support

Your response is important to your child's feelings of success. Keep your remarks positive. Recognize the effort your child has made. Correct mistakes together. Work toward independence, guiding practice when necessary.

Preparing to Read

Have your child look at the story.

- Ask, What do you think the story will be about?" (At this reading level the pictures provide important information to story meaning.)

- If your child does not mention the letter sound, point it out. Say, "This is a story for the letter *P*. Why do you think there's a pig on the page?"

Reading the Story

- Have your child point to the words on the page and read them aloud to you. Help as needed. Have your child read and reread favorite stories.

- Talk about what's happening.

- Have your child
  - retell the story using the pictures, or
  - tell what might happen next, or
  - tell how the story is like something he or she has experienced.

Doing the Activity Pages

Help your child read the directions for each page. Have your child do the pages independently, if possible, then help him or her check the work.

Encourage independent reading in addition to the stories in *Reading Practice at Home*.

Be a Model

The most important thing you can do for your child is to read.

- Read to your child. Visit libraries and bookstores, and don't forget to read your way through museums, parks, stores, and playgrounds.

- Read by yourself. It is important for your child to see you reading. Read books, magazines, and newspapers. Read signs, labels, letters, directions, and displays as well.

Read Your Environment

Beginning readers learn by reading the familiar words around them.

- Point out signs or trademarks that your child knows. Say, "Look at the sign on that restaurant. What does it say?"

- Applaud successful reading. Say, "You're right. That sign says 'Exit.'"

- Cut out familiar words from advertisements. Glue the print onto a piece of cardboard or put it in a scrapbook. Read the words often.

Help Your Child Select Appropriate Books for Additional Reading

Use the "five finger" method in picking out a book at an appropriate level. Have your child read a page from the book, raising a finger for each word he or she doesn't know. If no fingers are raised, the book may be too easy. If all five fingers are raised before the end of the page, the book is probably too difficult. This doesn't mean your child shouldn't read the book. It does mean that someone will need to be available to assist with difficult words.

Using the Practice Cards

Letter Identification

Name the Letter
Hold up one card at a time. Have your child name the letter.

Match Upper- and Lowercase Letters
Place all the cards on a flat surface. Have your child match all the capital and lowercase letters.

Alphabetical Order

Put Them in Order
Sing the alphabet song with your child and practice putting the letter cards in order as you sing.

Before or After?
Choose a letter card. Have your child choose another card and tell whether the letter on the card comes before or after the letter on your card in alphabetical order. *Note:* You may need to sing the alphabet song over and over for this activity. That's good practice!

Letter/Sound Associations

The Same Sound
Have your child choose a picture. Ask, "Can you think of other things that begin with the same sound?" (dog—*donut, dish, doctor*)

Match 'Em Up!
Choose a picture card. Say the name of the picture. Have your child say the name after you. Ask your child, "What letter stands for the sound you hear at the beginning of _____?" Isolate the sound if necessary so that your child can hear the sound clearly. ("What letter stands for the sound you hear at the beginning of dog? /d/— dog")

Color and Number Words

Read the Word

Hold up a word. Have your child read the word. Make two piles: "I can read these!" and "I'll practice these."

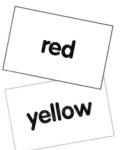

Funny Pictures

Combine color and number cards with picture cards to make a phrase. Then have your child read the cards and draw a picture that shows the meaning. *Six purple dogs.*

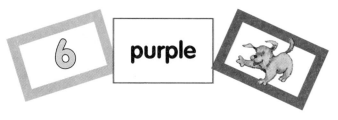

Storytelling

A New Story

Choose a picture and tell a story about the picture.

(pig—*Percy the pig lived in a little house by a mud puddle. His most favorite thing in the world was mud….*) Take turns with your child.

Adding On

Begin by telling a story about one picture and then choose a new picture. Add on to the story to accommodate the new character. Take turns choosing pictures and adding on.

Write It Down!

Write down the stories as they're told! Encourage your child to illustrate each story. Keep the stories and reread them often.

Spelling

Spell It!

Use the letter cards to spell a name or a favorite word. Copy the word on a paper.

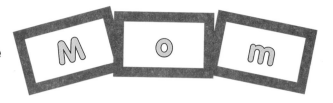

How Many?

See how many different names and words you can spell.

Any Ants?

1 ant

2 ants

ants in
my pants

Aa

Listen for the Sound

Color the pictures that begin like ant.

Aa

Reading Practice at Home • EMC 4510

What Does It Say?

Match the word to the picture.

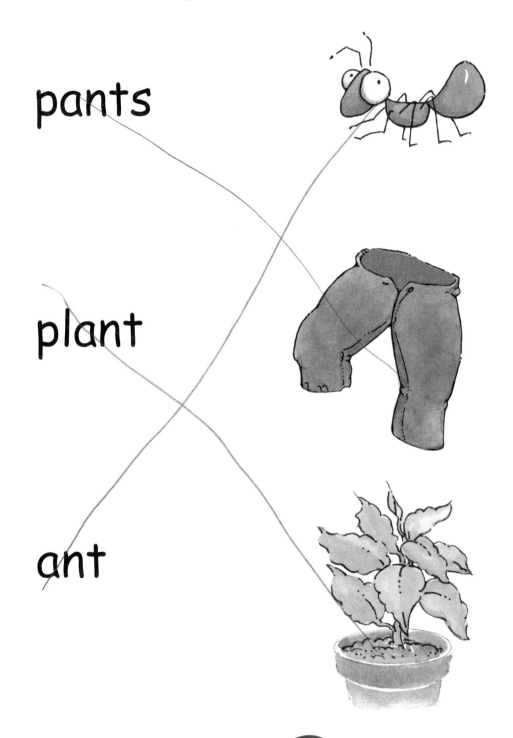

pants

plant

ant

How Many?

Cut and paste to tell how many.

1 ant

2 ants

3 ants

4 ants

5 ants

6 ants

paste

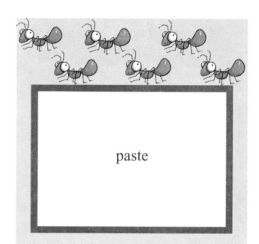

paste

paste

paste

paste

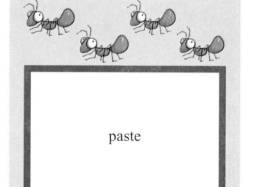

paste

Draw It!

1. Draw 1 red ant.

3. Draw ants on the pants.

2. Draw 2 green ants.

Aa

Bouncing Balls

big ball   little ball

See the balls.

Bb

     Reading Practice at Home • EMC 4510

Listen for the Sound

Color the pictures that begin with the same sound as ball.

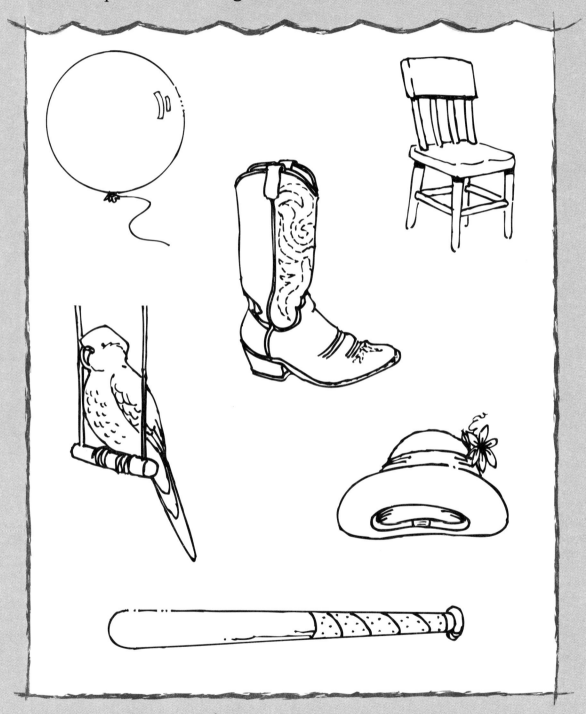

Bb

box

bed

bat

ball

What Does It Say?

Cut and paste to name each picture. Color the pictures.

paste

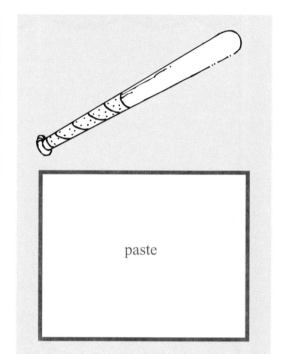

paste

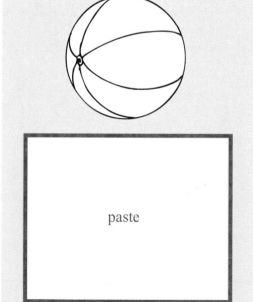

paste

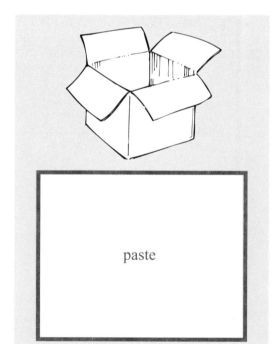

paste

Bb

Reading Practice at Home • EMC 4510

Big or Little?

Draw 3 **big** things here.

Draw 3 **little** things here.

Seeing Shapes

Color the ○ ▬▬▬ .
Color the △ ▬▬▬ .
Color the □ ▬▬▬ .

14 ©2000 by Evan-Moor Corp.   Reading Practice at Home • EMC 4510

What Color Is It?

a red car

It's red.

a blue cup

It's blue.

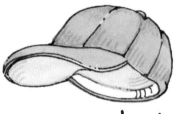

a green hat

It's green.

a yellow cat

It's yellow.

Cc

What Does It Say?

Draw a picture to show what the word says.

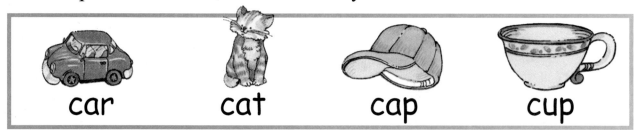

car   cat   cap   cup

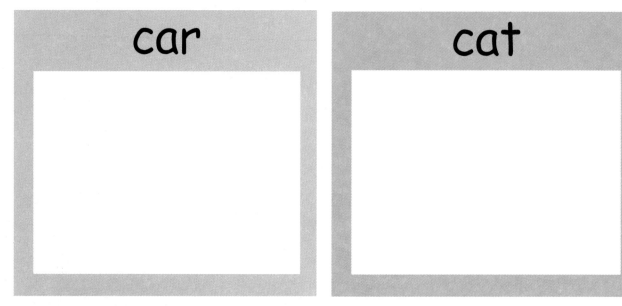

car

cat

cap

cup

     Reading Practice at Home • EMC 4510

Listen for the Sound

Cut and paste the pictures that begin with the same sound as car.

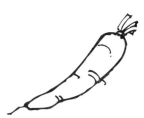

paste

paste

paste

paste

paste

CC

Color the Cat

Trace and write.

cat cat

Cc

Reading Practice at Home • EMC 4510

In the Cage

Connect the dots to finish the cage. Start with 1.

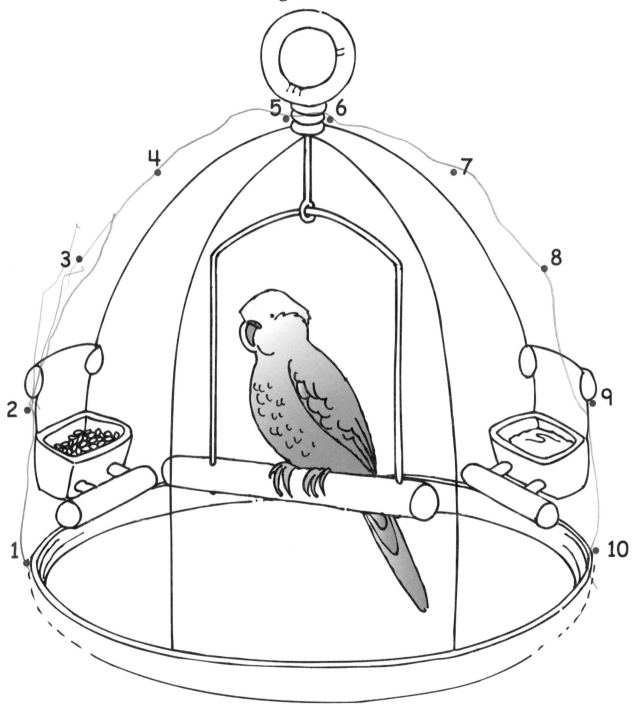

Digging

Dig, Dog, dig.

Dig, Dog, dig.

Dd

Listen for the Sound

Color the pictures that begin with the same sound as dog.

Dd

What Does It Say?

Draw a line to the right animal.

dog

cat

mouse

horse

frog

Dudley Duck

Trace the – – – – lines. Color the picture.

A Good Place to Dig

Circle yes or no.

This is a good place to dig.
yes   no

This is a good place to dig.
yes   no

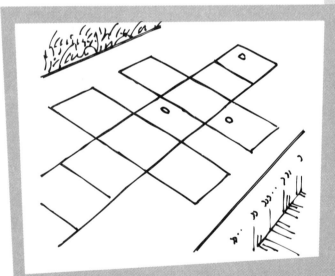

This is a good place to dig.
yes   no

This is a good place to dig.
yes   no

Dd

Eggs

big eggs

little eggs

pretty eggs

Ee

Listen for the Sound

Color the pictures that begin with the same sound as egg.
Make an **X** on the pictures that begin with a different sound.

Ee

Seeing Words

Circle the words that are the same as the first word in each row.

egg	egg	eagle	egg
big	dig	big	big
little	little	little	lift
candy	dandy	candy	candy
good	good	dog	good

Ee

What Does It Say?

Circle the word that names the picture.

	ball	rug
	pen	cat
	egg	leg
	book	ant
	dog	moon
	sun	cap

Ee

   Reading Practice at Home • EMC 4510

Is It Real?

Circle yes or no.

Is it real?

yes   **no**

Is it real?

yes   **no**

Is it real?

yes   **no**

Is it real?

yes   **no**

Ee

Swim, Fish, Swim

Little fish, little fish,
Swish, swish, swish.

Ff

     Reading Practice at Home • EMC 4510

Listen for the Sound

Cut and paste to show which pictures begin with the same sound as fish.

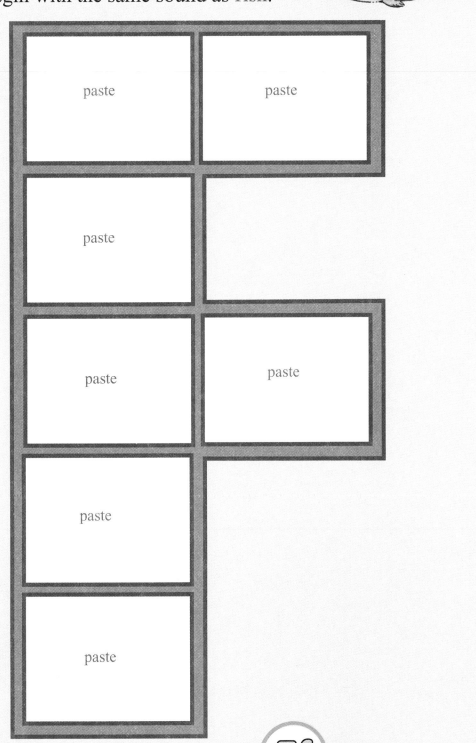

paste	paste
paste	
paste	paste
paste	
paste	

Ff

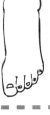

What Does It Say?

Color the fish.

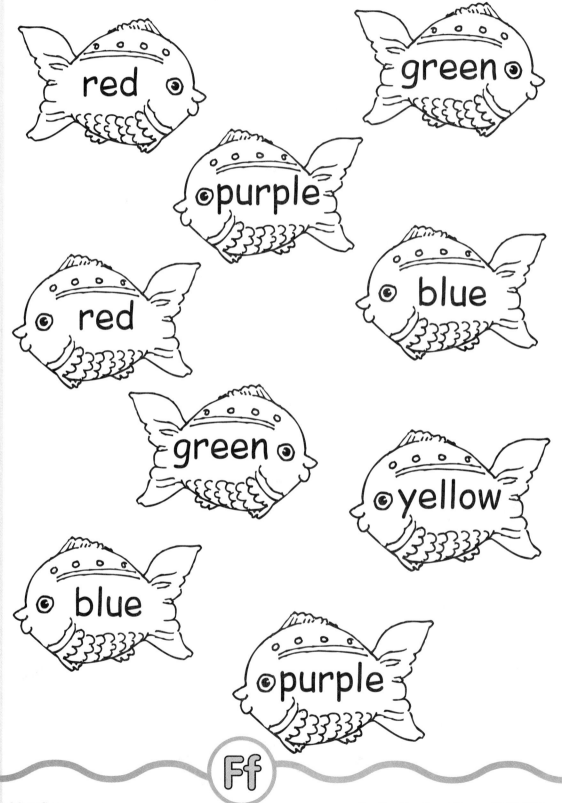

red

green

purple

red

blue

green

yellow

blue

purple

Ff

Rhyme Time

Circle the pictures in each line that rhyme.

How Many?

Write the number to tell how many.

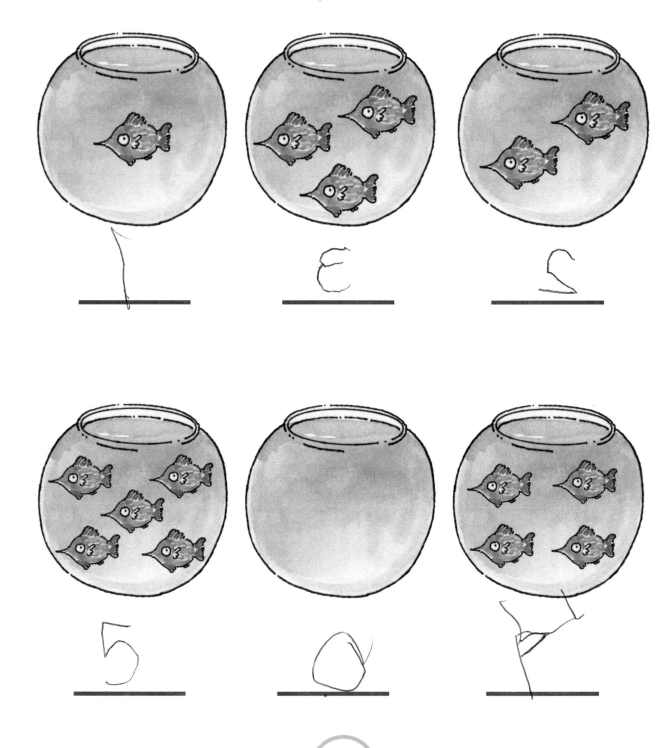

Good!

Bad!

Good!

Bad!

What a day I had!

Gg

Listen for the Sound

Color the pictures that begin with the sound that **g** makes in goat.

Gg

Put It in Order

Color, cut, and paste. Put the pictures in order.

1

paste

2

paste

3

paste

4

paste

Gg

G at the End

Circle the pictures that have the sound of **g** at the end.

Gg

   Reading Practice at Home • EMC 4510

What Do You Think?

Trace.

good   bad

Write good or bad.

_____   _____

Gg

Hippo's Hat

one hat
one big hat
one big red hat

Hh

Listen for the Sound

Circle the pictures that begin with the same sound as hippo.

What Does It Say?

Draw a picture to show what each word means.

hat

rat

cat

bat

mat

flat

Hh

The House on the Hill

Follow the dots to make a hill.
Color the hill.
Draw a house on top.

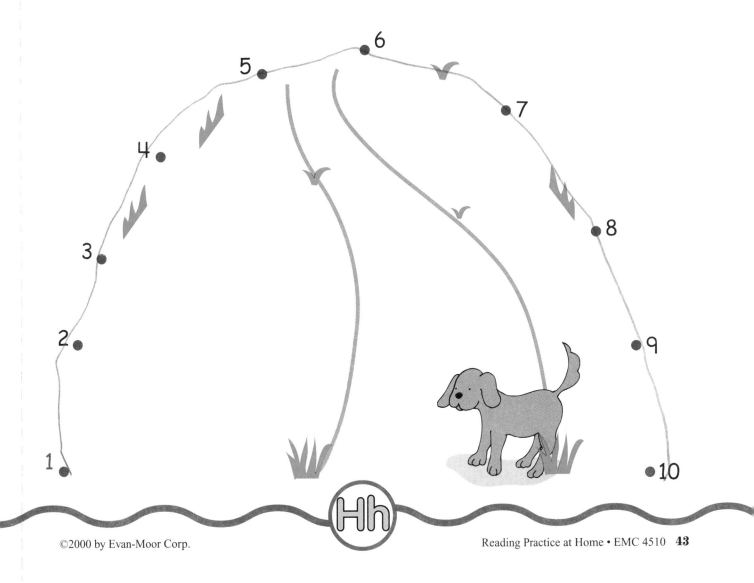

What's Inside?

Lift the lid.
See what hid.

in a box

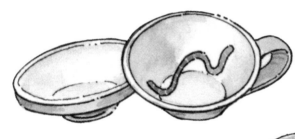 in a cup

in a jar

Close it up!

Ii

Is He Happy?

Circle yes or no.

Is he happy?  yes
no

Is he happy?  yes
no

Is he happy?  yes
no

Is he happy?  yes
no

What Can You Do?

Read the words. Draw a picture to show what they say.

I can stop.

I can go.

©2000 by Evan-Moor Corp.

Reading Practice at Home • EMC 4510

Interesting Insects!

Color, cut, and paste. Put the insects in the jar.

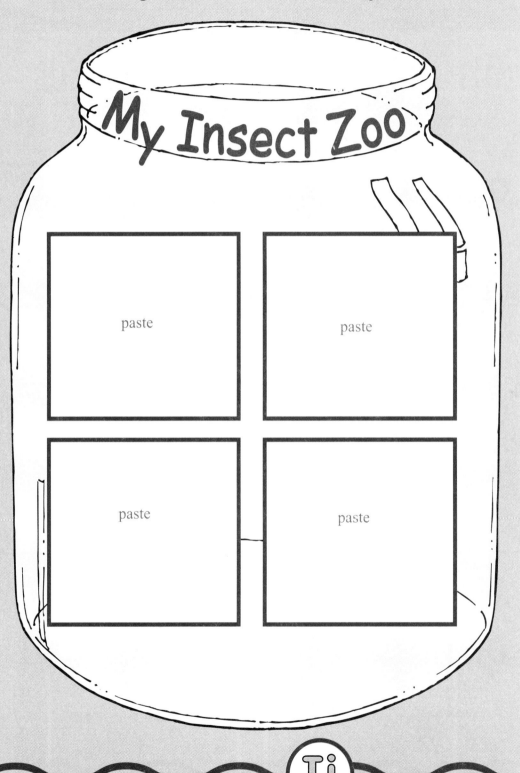

In or Out?

Where is it? Circle **in** or **out**.

in

out

in

out

in

out

in

out

in

out

in

out

Find the Words

Circle the words that are the same in each row.

| big | big | dig | big |

| pig | dig | pig | pig |

| wig | wig | wig | mig |

| kick | lick | kick | kick |

| sick | sick | slick | sick |

| hill | hall | hill | hill |

Just a Jar

What's in the jar?

jam

What's in the jar?

jelly beans

What's in the jar?

June bug

Listen for the Sound

Color, cut, and paste. Put all the pictures that begin with the sound of **j** in the letter.

paste

paste

paste

paste

paste

What Does It Say?

Match the word to the picture. Color the pictures.

jar

jam

jet

jeep

Jj

                          Reading Practice at Home • EMC 4510

How Many Balls?

Color. Count. Write the number word to tell how many.

_____ balls

_____ balls

_____ balls

_____ balls

Word Box

one	two	three	four	five	six

Jj

Just Jack

Color all the pieces of the puzzle that have a dot.

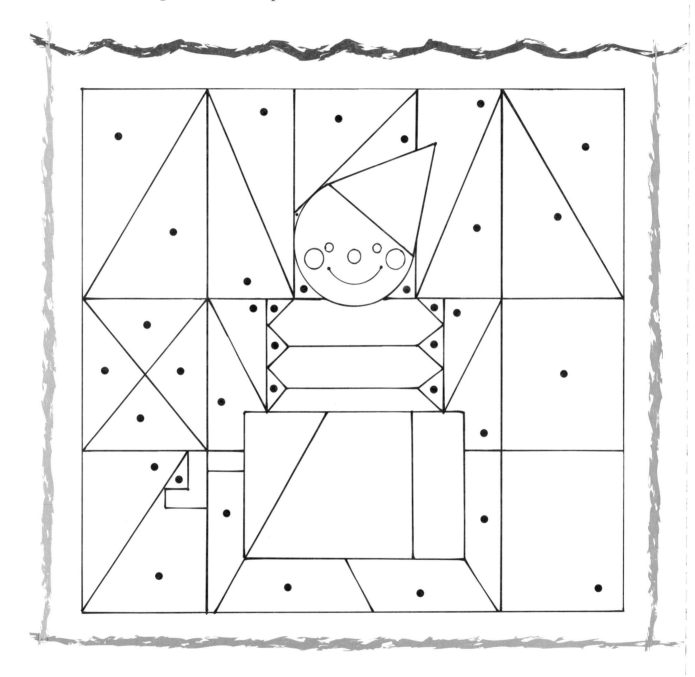

See Jack.

    Reading Practice at Home • EMC 4510

Important Keys

Lock it up!

a key for the suitcase

Lock it up!

a key for the door

Start it up!

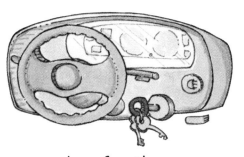
a key for the car

Here we go!

Kk

Listen for the Sound

Circle the pictures that begin with the same sound as key.

Kk

Kites, Kites, Kites

Read the color words. Color the kites.

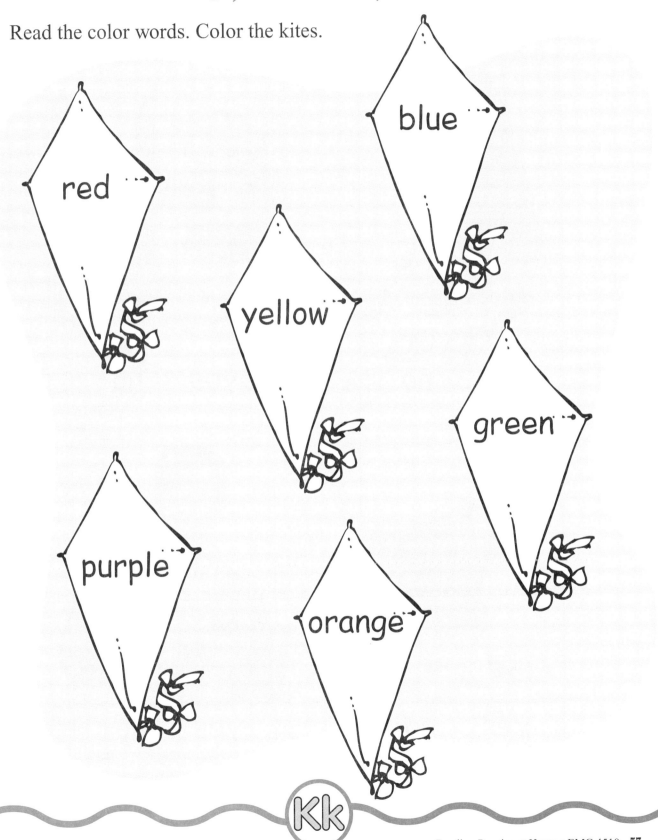

©2000 by Evan-Moor Corp.   Reading Practice at Home • EMC 4510   **57**

Kindergarten

Could it happen in kindergarten? Circle yes or no.

yes   no

yes   no

yes   no

yes   no

Kk

New Words

The pictures show what each new **k** word means. Draw a line to show who would use each thing.

kennel

kerchief

kettle

kayak

Kk

Let's Go to the Zoo

Look!

a lion

a llama

a leopard

a lollipop

Ll

Reading Practice at Home • EMC 4510

Listen for the Sound

Say the name of each picture. Do you hear the l sound first or last?

first last	first last	first last
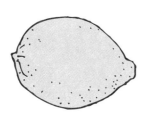	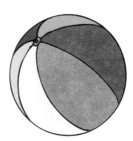	
first last	first last	first last

first last	first last	first last

Ll

Little or Large?

Color the pictures. Put an **X** on the little one.

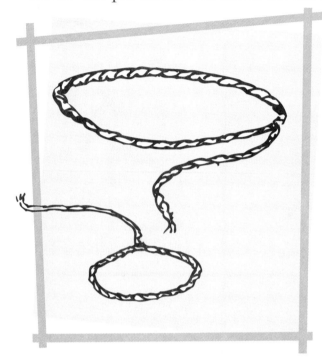

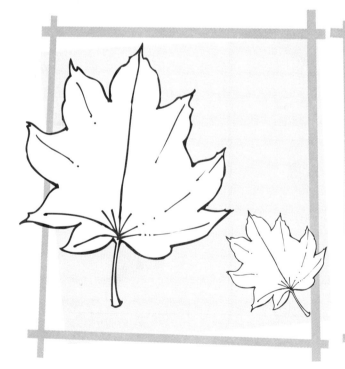

Reading Practice at Home • EMC 4510

Look! I can make new words!

Start with look.

l o o k

Take off the l.
Put on a b.

__ o o k

Take off the b.
Put on an h.

__ o o k

Take off the h.
Put on a c.

__ o o k

Take off the c.
Put on br.

__ __ o o k

©2000 by Evan-Moor Corp.

What's for Lunch?

Color the food.

Reading Practice at Home • EMC 4510

Special Places

Little mouse
has a house.

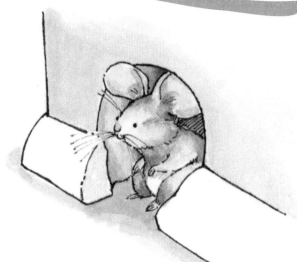

Little mole
has a hole.

Little me
in a tepee.

Listen for the Sound

Color the pictures that begin with the same sound as mouse.

Mail

Mm

Match the Mittens

Cut and paste to make pairs.

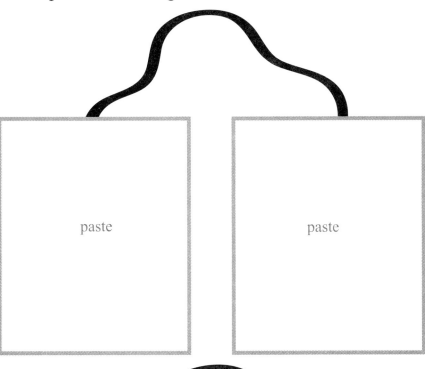

paste paste

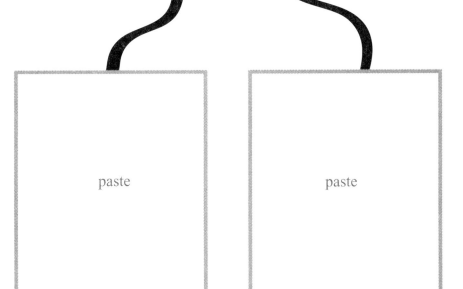

paste paste

Mm

What Sound Does It Make?

Match the picture and the sound.

Meow

Moo

Brrmmmmm

Mama Mama

In the Night Sky

Connect the dots. Start with 1. Color the picture.

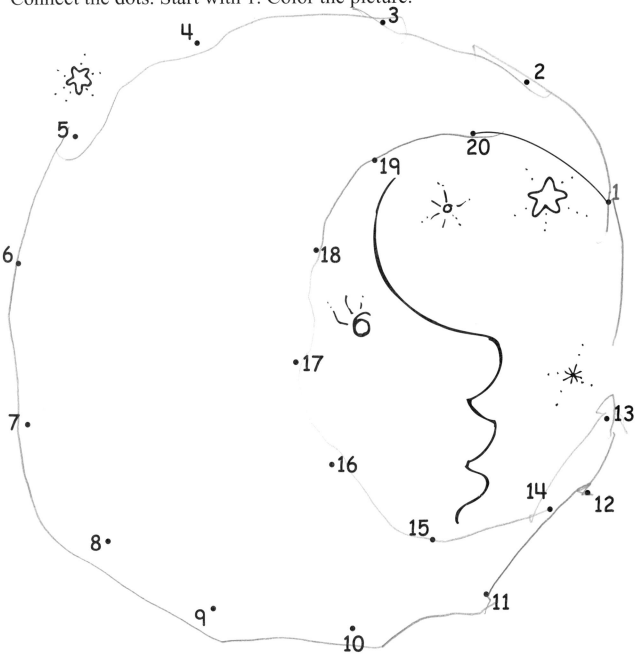

Have you ever seen the moon?

yes   no

The New One

Is it in the nest?

No

Is it in the net?

No

It's in the nursery!

Nn

Listen for the Sound

Cut and paste to show what pictures begin with the same sound as net.

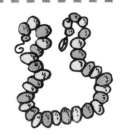

paste

paste

paste

paste

paste

Nn

No, No, No

Write No or Yes.

 The ball is red. _____

 The ball is green. _____

 The ball is yellow. _____

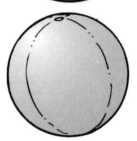 The ball is brown. _____

Do you have a ball? _____

Do you play with a ball? _____

Nn

Noodle Necklace

Cut and paste. Make a necklace.

paste

paste

paste

paste

paste

paste

paste

paste

paste

Nn

Naughty or Nice?

Circle the word to tell whether they are naughty or nice.

naughty   nice

naughty   nice

naughty   nice

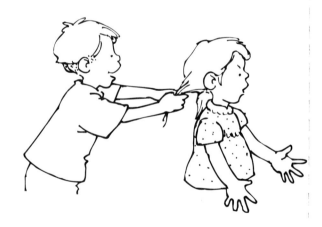

naughty   nice

Nn

This is an otter.
It lives in the water.

This is an ostrich.
It lives on the land.

Oo

Listen for the Sound

Color the pictures that begin like otter.

Making New Words

Add a letter to **-and** to make a new word that tells what the picture is.

___and   ___and   ___and

Write one of the new words in each sentence.

Dump the _____.

Wash your _____.

Hear the _____.

Make Them Look the Same

Look at the first thing. Make the others the same.

Rhyme Time

Color the pictures that rhyme with frog.

 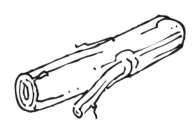 

Color the pictures that rhyme with rock.

Color the pictures that rhyme with top.

In a Puddle

The puppy's in a puddle.

The pig's in a puddle.

I'm in a puddle, too.

Pp

     Reading Practice at Home • EMC 4510

Listen for the Sound

Color the pictures to show the words that begin with the sound that p stands for.

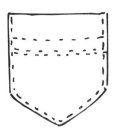

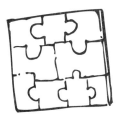

Pp

What Does It Say?

The  is **on** the pot.

The  is **by** the pot.

The  is **in** the pot.

The  is **under** the pot.

Pp

In the Pen

Draw: one pink pig

two black sheep

three yellow chicks

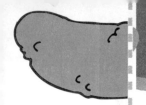

Puzzles, Puzzles, Puzzles

Put the puzzles together. Answer yes or no.

Do you like pickles?

yes   no

paste	paste

paste	paste

Do you like popcorn?

yes   no

Do you like pancakes?

yes   no

paste	paste

paste	paste

Do you like pizza?

yes   no

Be Quiet!

Quack, quack, quack.

Be quiet!

Quack, quack, quack.

Be quiet!

Quack, quack, quack.

Quiet!

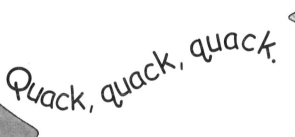

Qq

Listen for the Sound

Color the pictures that have the same beginning sound as quack.

Quack

Qq

Reading Practice at Home • EMC 4510

What Does It Say?

Match.

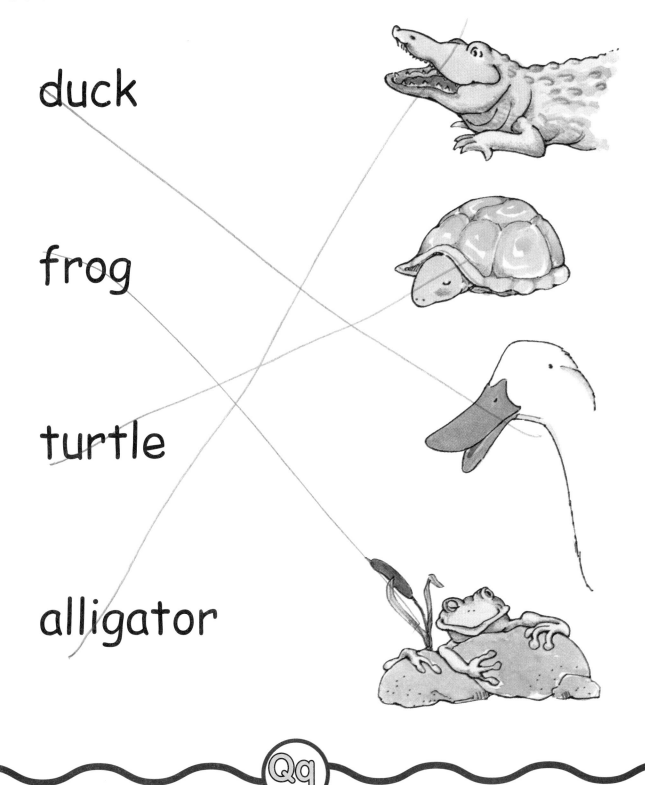

duck

frog

turtle

alligator

A Quiet Time

Find these things. Color them.

Reading Practice at Home • EMC 4510

Seeing Words

Circle the words that are the same as the first word in each row.

jump	jump	run	jump
sleep	slip	sleep	sleep
quack	quack	quack	quiet
sit	sip	sit	sit
dog	dog	bog	dog
home	home	house	home

Run, rabbit, run.

Run, rooster, run.

Run, rhinoceros, run.

What a race!

Rr

Listen for the Sound

Cut and paste to show which pictures begin with the same sound as rabbit.

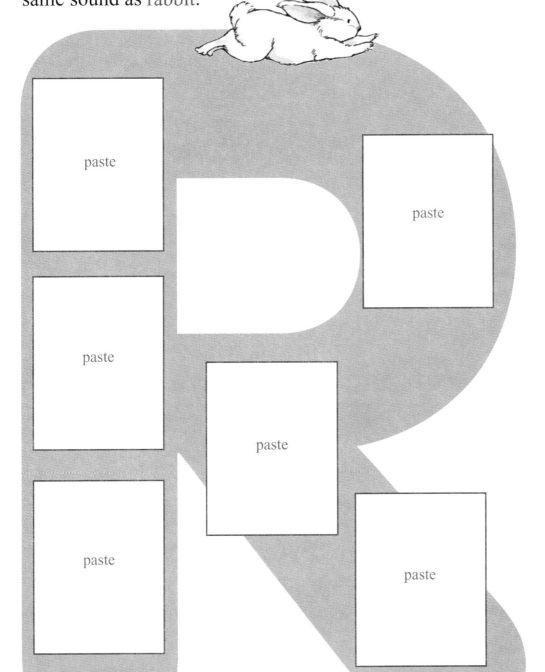

paste

paste

paste

paste

paste

paste

Rr

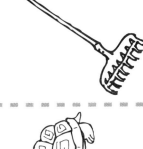

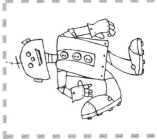

What Does It Say?

Draw a line from the sentence to the correct picture.

I can run.

I can rest.

I can read.

Draw It!

Draw and color. Give the robot a name.

Find the Rhyme

Circle the pictures in each row that rhyme.

Reading Practice at Home • EMC 4510

Sad Sam

See Sam.
Sam is sad.

See Sam.
Sam is so sad.
Sad, sad Sam.

Ss

Listen for the Sound

6

Color the pictures that begin with the same sound as six.

What Does It Say?

Circle the word that tells about the picture. Write the word in the sentence.

sad   glad

Sam is _____.

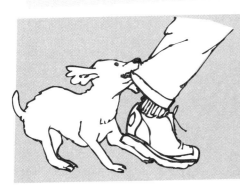

mad   sad

The dog is _____.

Bad   Dad

_____ kitty!

sad   glad

Sam is _____.

Ss

More Than One

Add **s** to the end of the word to mean more than one. Color the pictures.

1 sock

3 sock___

1 sub

2 sub___

1 star

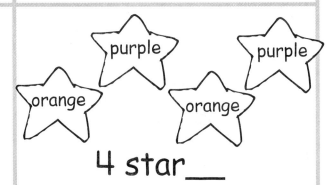

4 star___

1 spoon

2 spoon___

Dot-to-Dot

Connect the dots. Start with 1.

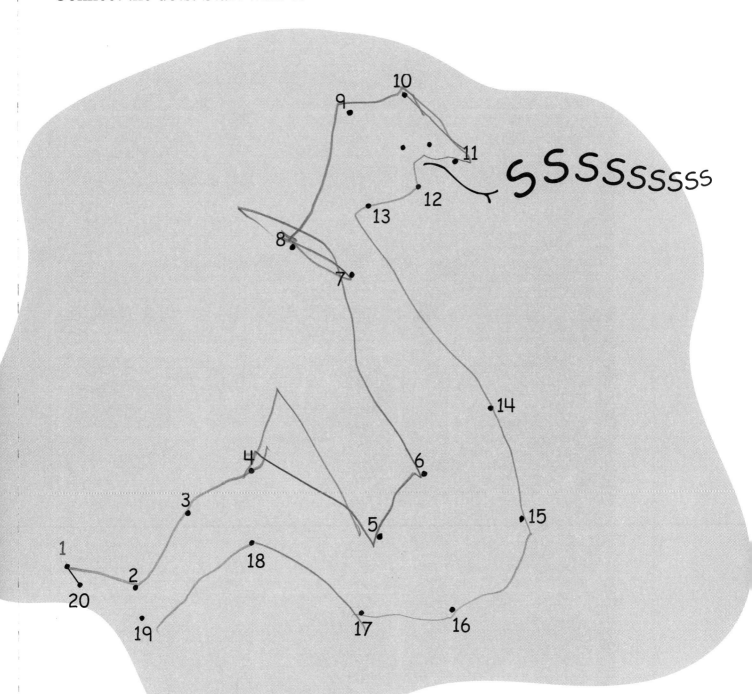

SSSSSsssss

On the Trail

2 turtles in a tent.

2 turtles at the table.

2 turtles go to town.

2 tired turtles!

Tt

    Reading Practice at Home • EMC 4510

Listen for the Sound

Cut and paste the pictures that begin with the same sound as tent.

paste

paste

paste

paste

paste

paste

paste

paste

Tt

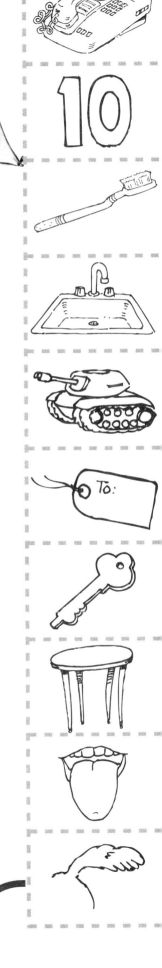

First or Last?

Say the name of each picture. Circle first or last to tell where you hear the **t** sound.

first   last

first   last

first   last

first   last

first   last

first   last

first   last

first   last

first   last

Tt

Reading Practice at Home • EMC 4510

What Does It Say?

Color the animals. Finish the name of each animal.

__a__   __o__   __u__

__i__   __e__   __if__

Circle the animals that have 4 legs.

What Will Come Next?

Circle the picture that shows what will happen next.

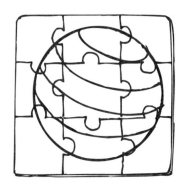

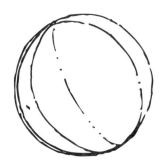

Tt

Up, up, up, up, up, up.

Down!

Uu

Listen for the Sound

Color the pictures that begin with the same sound as umbrella.
Circle the one that is under in each picture.

Uu

Up or Down?

Write up or down.

_____

_____

_____

_____

Uu

Who Is Under the Umbrella?

Draw a line to show who is under the umbrella.

Read and Color

Read the words. Color the umbrella.

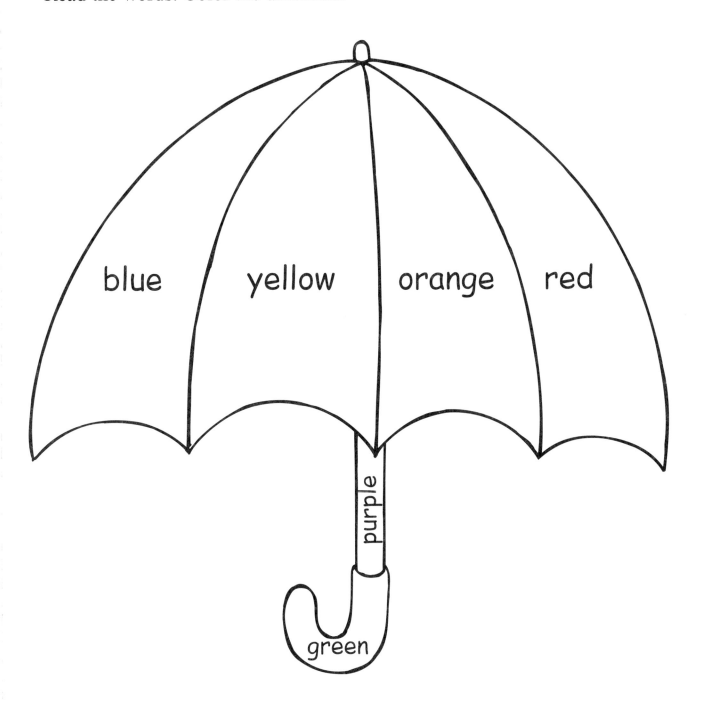

Very Nice!

See my vest.
It's the best.

Very nice.

See my van.
It is tan.

Very nice.

See my vine.
It's just fine.

Very nice.

Vv

Listen for the Sound

Cut and paste to show which pictures begin with the same sound as vine.

paste

paste

paste

paste

paste

paste

Vv

In the Garden

Color the vegetables.
Circle the one you like the very best.

red

yellow

orange

purple

green

brown

Vv

What Does It Say?

Draw a line from the word to the picture.

van

cave

vest

hive

stove

vase

Vv

Draw It!

Draw and color.

Waffle Wagon

What's in the wagon?

weeds

What's in the wagon?

water

What's in the wagon?

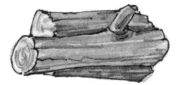

wood

What's in the wagon?

Waffles!

Ww

Listen for the Sound

Color the pictures that begin with the same sound as wagon.

Ww

What Does It Say?

Draw what you should do.

Walk

Wait

Seeing Words

Circle the words in each row that are the same as the first word.

with	with	will	with	with

went	won	went	went	went

was	was	was	saw	was

what	when	what	what	what

wish	wish	wish	wash	wish

wag	wag	wag	nag	wag

    Reading Practice at Home • EMC 4510

Make a Wish

Follow the dots. Start with 1.

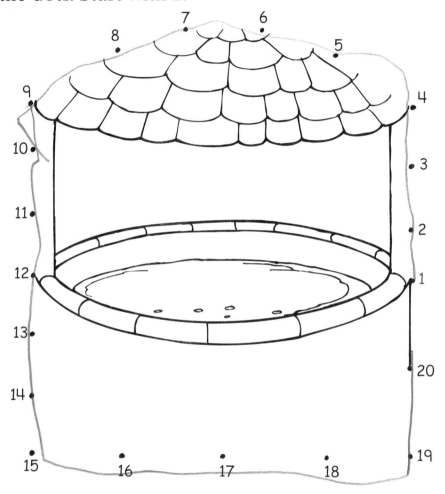

Have you made a wish at a wishing well?

yes   no

What did you wish for?

Fix It, Please!

Take an x-ray.

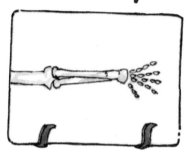  

Exit here.

Take an x-ray.

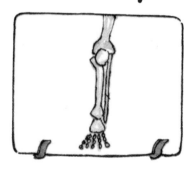 

Exit here.

Take an x-ray.

Exit here.

Xx

Listen for the Sound

Color the pictures that have the same ending sound as fox.
Write the end letter of each word.

bo___

a___

ca___

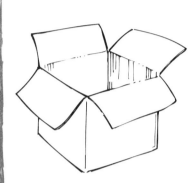

o___

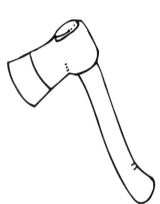

si___

do___

Xx

What Does It Say?

Color the spaces with dots to read the sign.

Follow the Directions

See the box.

Draw 3 balls in the box.

Color the balls blue.

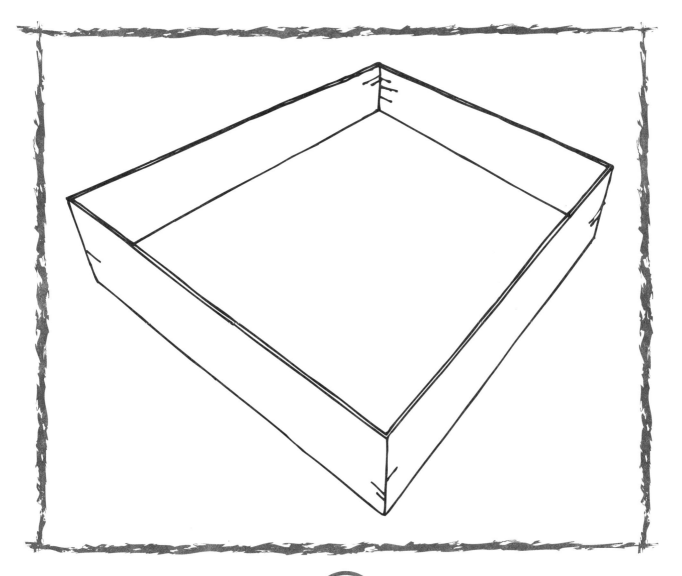

Rhyme Time

Circle the pictures that rhyme.

   Reading Practice at Home • EMC 4510

Time to Eat

Yum!

Yum!

Yuck!

Yy

Answer the Questions

Answer the questions. Write **yes** or **no**.

Do you like  ? _____

Do you like  ? _____

Do you like  ? _____

Do you like  ? _____

Do you like  ? _____

Do you like  ? _____

Yy

  Reading Practice at Home • EMC 4510

Listen for the Sound

Cut and paste to show the pictures that begin with the same sound as yum.

yum

paste	paste
paste	paste

paste

paste

Yy

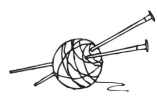

The -um Family

Write the words. Draw a line to the picture that matches.
Color the pictures.

g + um = _____

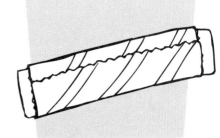

dr + um = _____

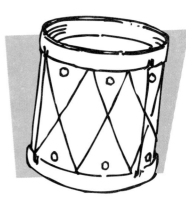

pl + um = _____

Yy

   Reading Practice at Home • EMC 4510

What Did Grandma Make?

Grandma made me a present. She made it out of yarn.
Color the shapes.

red = circles

blue = triangles

yellow = rectangles

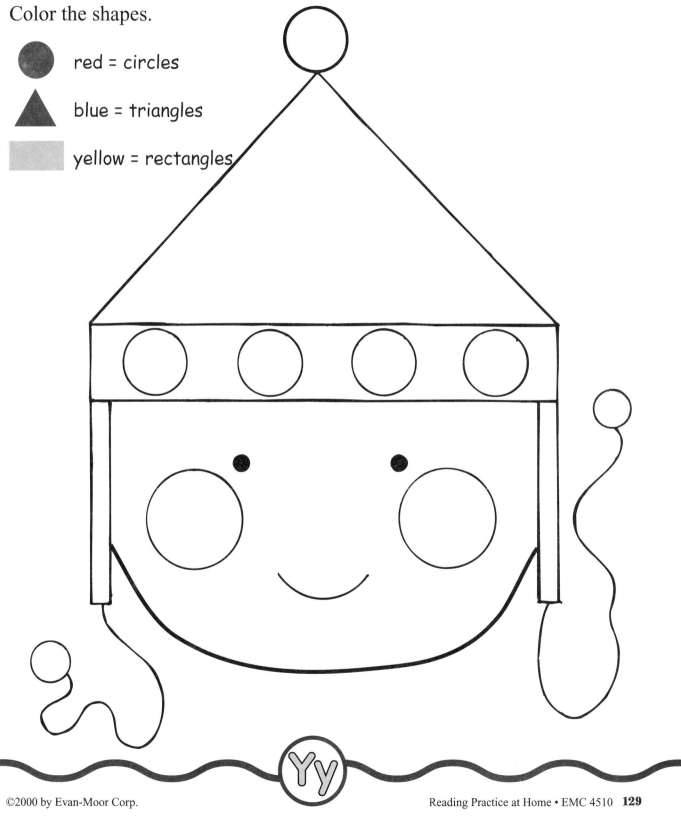

Beyond Zero

How many  ?

0   1   2

How many ?

0   1   2

How many  ?

0   1   2

Zillions!

Zz

Listen for the Sound

Color the pictures that begin with the same sound as zipper.

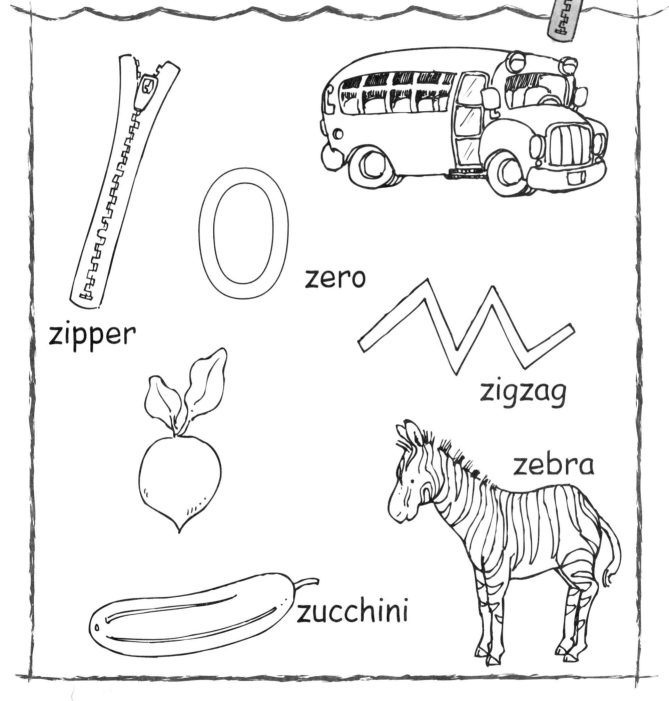

zipper

zero

zigzag

zebra

zucchini

Zz

Draw It!

Follow the steps. Make the race car zoom!

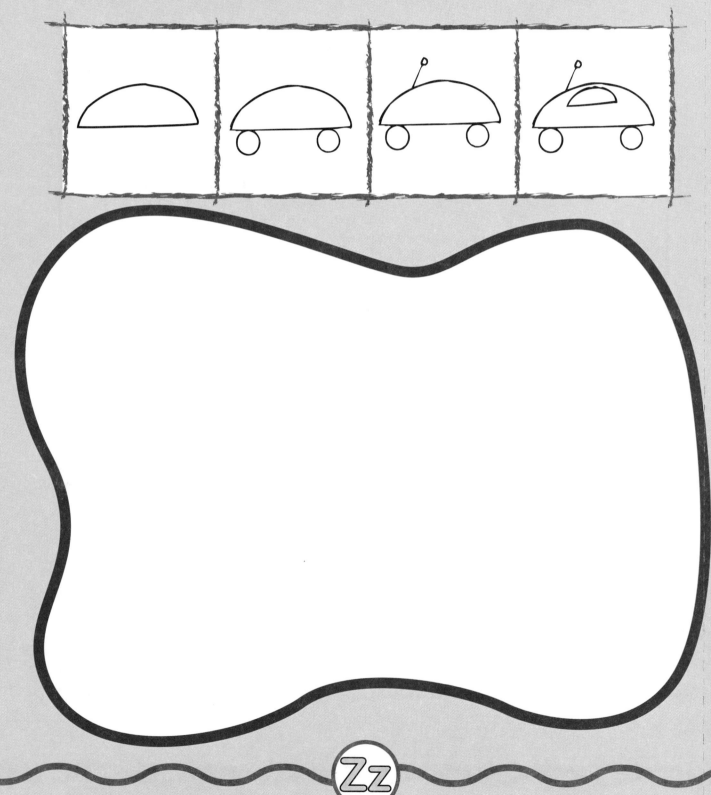

Seeing Words

Circle the words in each row that are the same as the first word.

| zip | zap | zip | zip | zip |

| zonk | zonk | honk | zonk | zonk |

| zany | zany | sany | zany | zany |

| zing | zing | zing | sing | zing |

| zap | lap | zap | zap | zap |

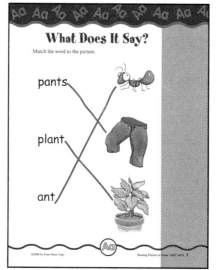

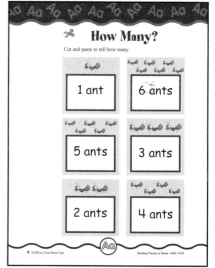

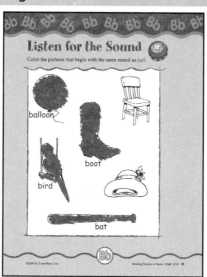

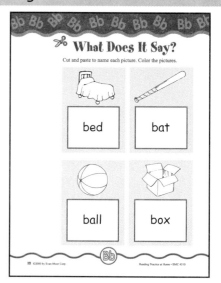

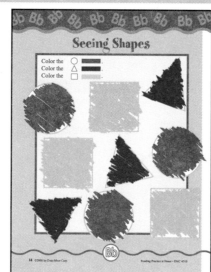

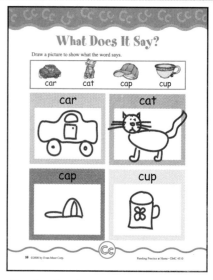

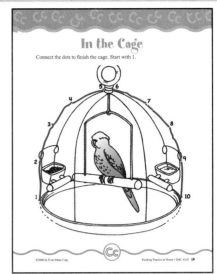

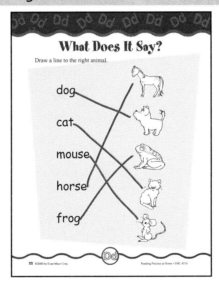

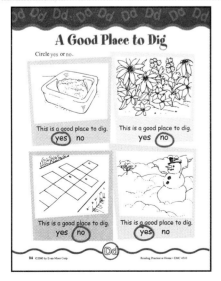

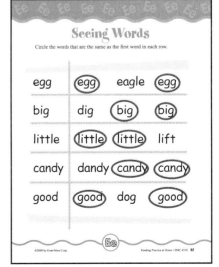

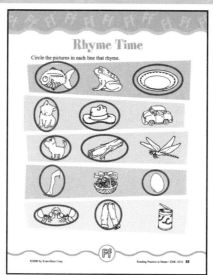

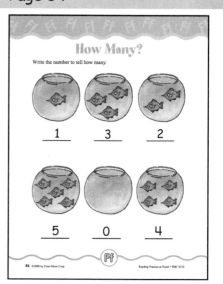

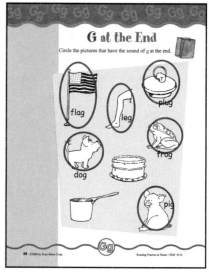

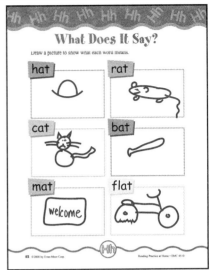

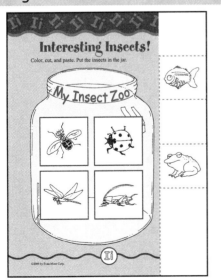

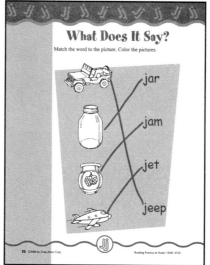

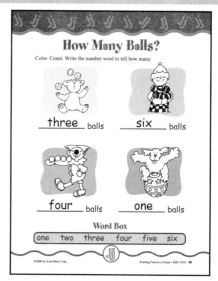

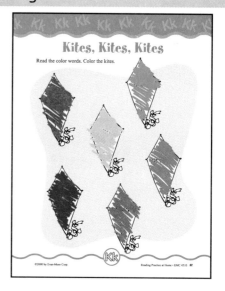

Page 62

Little or Large?
Color the pictures. Put an X on the little one.

Ll

Page 63

Look! I can make new words!

Start with look.	l o o k
Take off the l. Put on a b.	b o o k
Take off the b. Put on an h.	h o o k
Take off the h. Put on a c.	c o o k
Take off the c. Put on br.	b r o o k

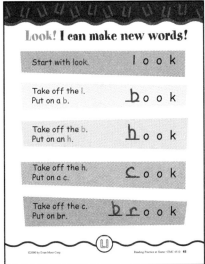

Ll

Page 64

What's for Lunch?
Color the food.

Ll

Page 66

Listen for the Sound
Color the pictures that begin with the same sound as mouse.

mail　mitten　moose　mouse　mitt　mask　monkey　map

Mm

Page 67

Match the Mittens
Cut and paste to make pairs.

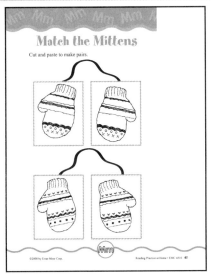

Mm

Page 68

What Sound Does It Make?
Match the picture and the sound.

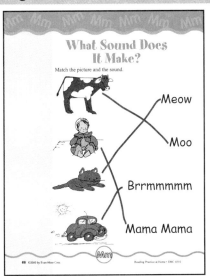

Meow

Moo

Brrmmmmm

Mama Mama

Mm

Page 69

In the Night Sky
Connect the dots. Start with 1. Color the picture.

Have you ever seen the moon?　Answers will vary.

yes　no

Mm

Page 71

Listen for the Sound
Cut and paste to show what pictures begin with the same sound as net.

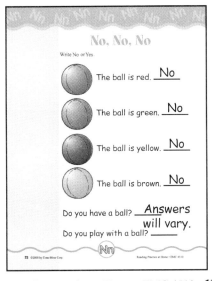

Nn

Page 72

No, No, No
Write No or Yes.

The ball is red. __No__

The ball is green. __No__

The ball is yellow. __No__

The ball is brown. __No__

Do you have a ball? __Answers will vary.__

Do you play with a ball? _____

Nn

Page 73

Noodle Necklace

Cut and paste. Make a necklace.

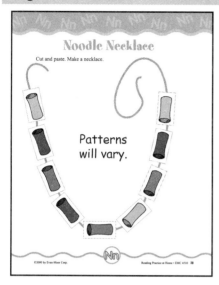

Patterns will vary.

Page 74

Naughty or Nice?

Circle the word to tell whether they are naughty or nice.

naughty (nice)   naughty (nice)

naughty (nice)   (naughty) nice

Page 76

Listen for the Sound

Color the pictures that begin like otter.

ostrich
otter
olive
octopus

Page 77

Making New Words

Add a letter to -and to make a new word that tells what the picture is.

h_and   s_and   b_and

Write one of the new words in each sentence.

Dump 🚚 the _sand_.

Wash your _hand_.

Hear the _band_.

Page 78

Make Them Look the Same

Look at the first thing. Make the others the same.

Page 79

Rhyme Time

Color the pictures that rhyme with frog.

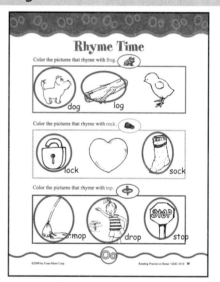

dog   log

Color the pictures that rhyme with rock.

lock   sock

Color the pictures that rhyme with top.

mop   drop   stop

Page 81

Listen for the Sound

Color the pictures to show the words that begin with the sound that p stands for.

pocket   potato   pencil
puzzle   popcorn   penny
pizza   pumpkin
pig   paint

Page 82

What Does It Say?

The ❤ is on the pot.

The 🥄 is by the pot.

The is in the pot.

The is under the pot.

Page 83

In the Pen

Draw: one pink pig
two black sheep
three yellow chicks

Drawings will vary. There should be 1 pig, 2 sheep, and 3 chicks.

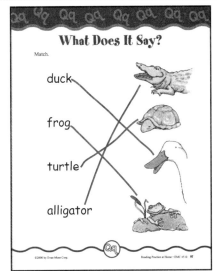

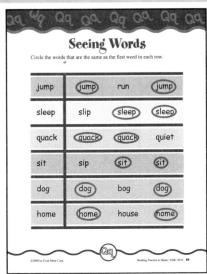

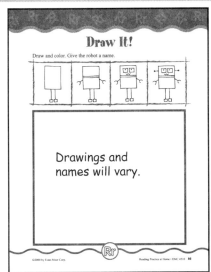

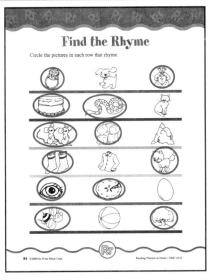

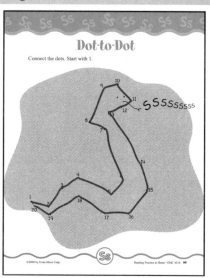

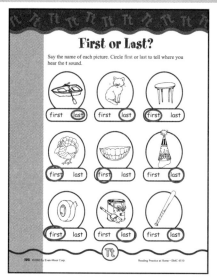

Page 107

Page 108

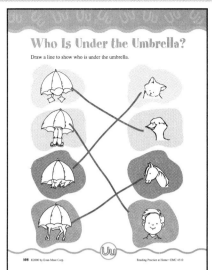

Page 109

Page 111

Page 112

Page 113

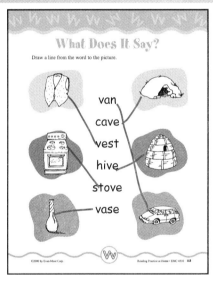

Page 116

Page 118

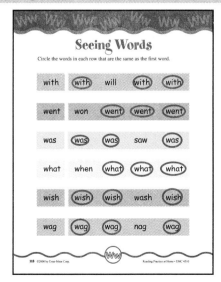

Page 119

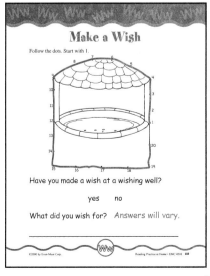

Listen for the Sound
Color the pictures that have the same ending sound as fox.
Write the end letter of each word.

bo X   a X   ca t

o X   si X   do g

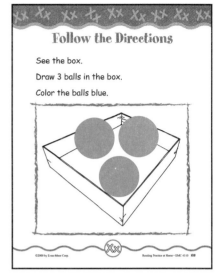

What Does It Say?
Color the spaces with dots to read the sign.

EXIT

Follow the Directions

See the box.

Draw 3 balls in the box.

Color the balls blue.

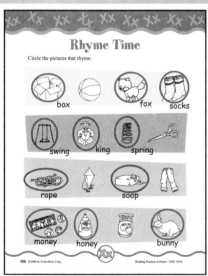

Rhyme Time
Circle the pictures that rhyme.

box   fox   socks

swing   king   spring

rope   soap

money   honey   bunny

Listen for the Sound
Cut and paste to show the pictures that begin with the same sound as yum.

yum

The -um Family
Write the words. Draw a line to the picture that matches.
Color the pictures.

g + um =   gum

dr + um =   drum

pl + um =   plum

What Did Grandma Make?
Grandma made me a present. She made it out of yarn.
Color the shapes.

red = circles

blue = triangles

yellow = rectangles

Listen for the Sound
Color the pictures that begin with the same sound as zipper.

zipper   zero   zigzag   zebra   zucchini

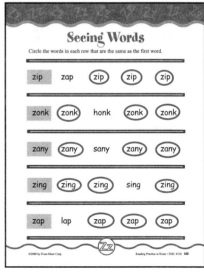

Seeing Words
Circle the words in each row that are the same as the first word.

zip	zap	zip	zip	zip
zonk	zonk	honk	zonk	zonk
zany	zany	sany	zany	zany
zing	zing	zing	sing	zing
zap	lap	zap	zap	zap

A a

B b

C c

D d

E   e

F   f

G   g

H   h

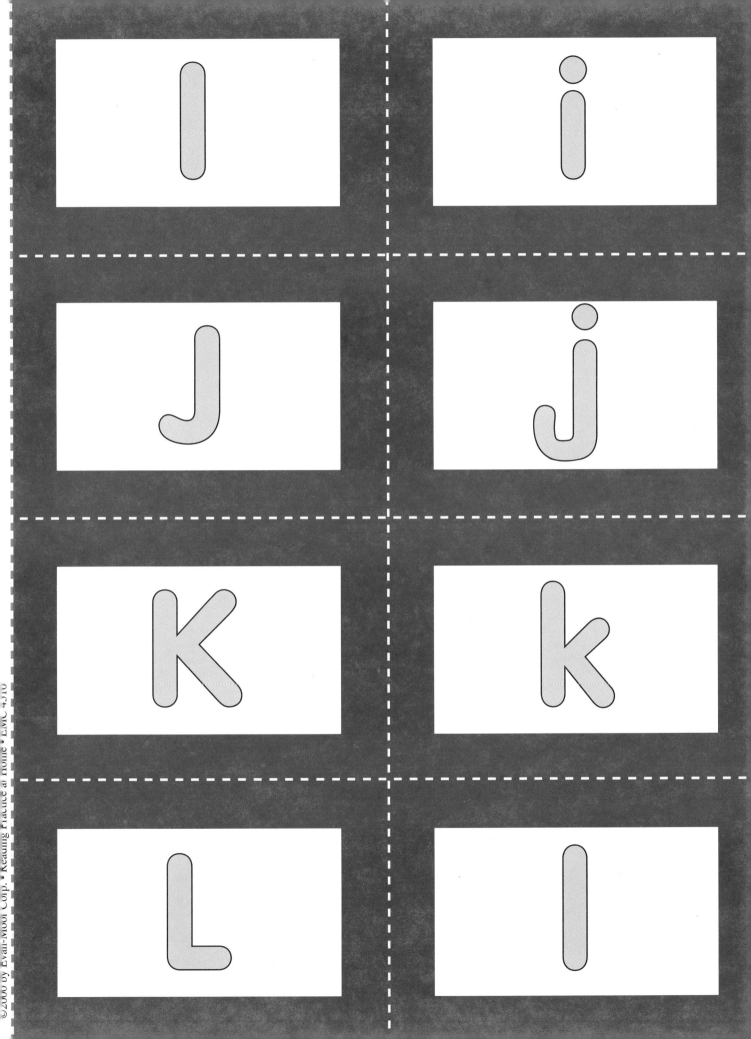

I i

J j

K k

L l

M

m

N

n

O

o

P

p

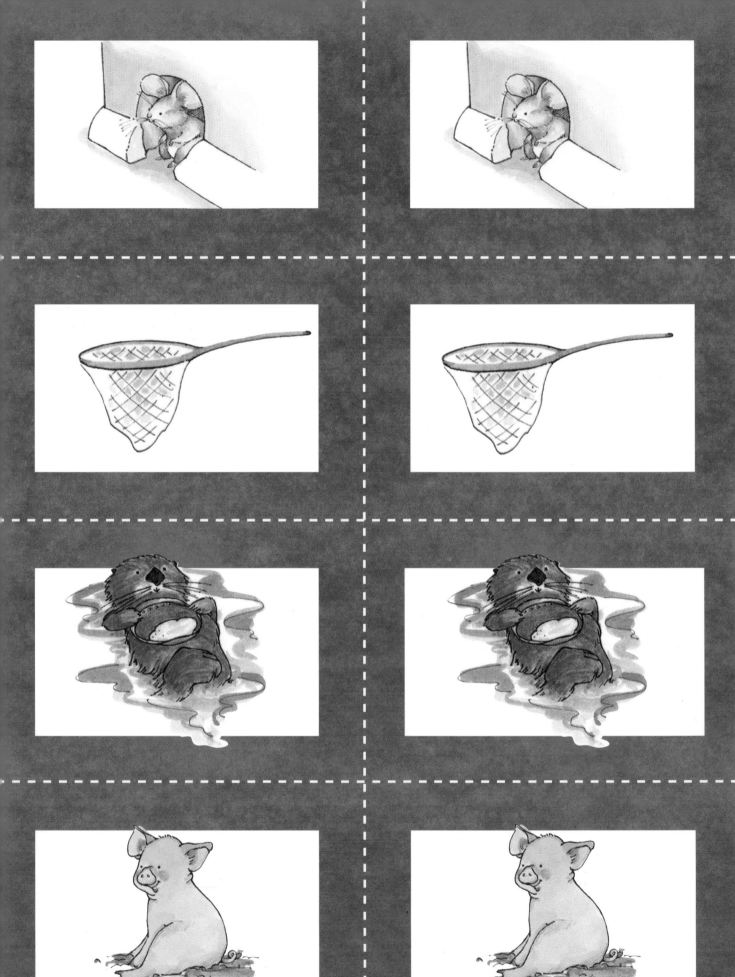

Q   q

R   r

S   s

T   t

 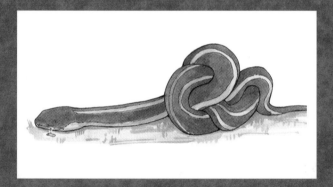

U

U

V

V

W

W

X

X

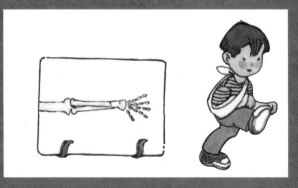 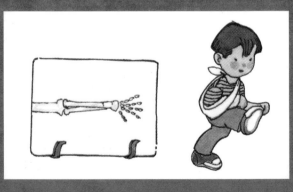

Y

y

Z

z

red

yellow

green

blue

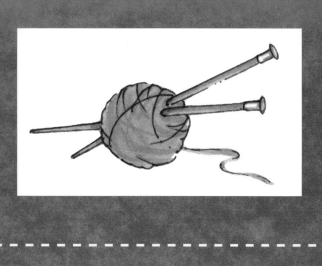

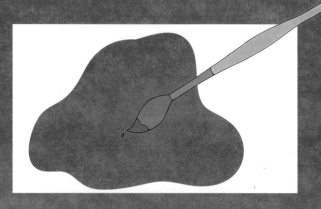
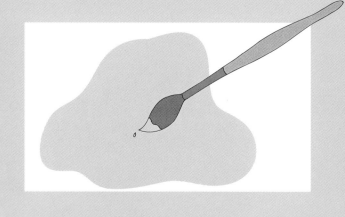
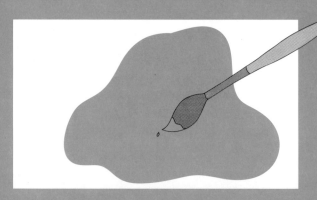
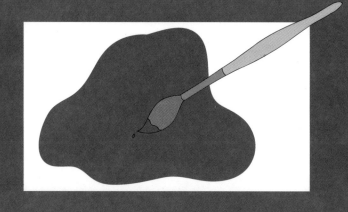

purple

orange

one

two

three

four

five

six

2

1

4

3

6

5